blur by the

Cham Zhi Yi

First published 2019
by Subbed In
www.subbed.in

© Cham Zhi Yi 2019

Book design by Michael Sun
Cover design by Dan Hogan
Cover artwork by Idezem via Openclipart.org (Creative Commons
Zero 1.0 Public Domain License)
Original template by Sam Wieck
Text set in 8pt Domaine Text

First edition

Printed and bound in Birraranga (Melbourne)

National Library of Australia Cataloguing-in-Publication:
Zhi Yi, Cham
blur by the / Cham Zhi Yi.
ISBN: 978-0-6481475-4-1 (paperback)

Subbed In 005

All rights reserved.

This book is copyright. Apart from any fair dealing for the purposes of
research, criticism, study, review or otherwise permitted under the
Copyright Act, no part of this book may be reproduced by any process
without permission. Inquiries should be addressed to Subbed In:
hello@subbed.in

I want so badly to transform
but everyone is watching
— *Saaro Umar,*
　from the poem 'Gotu Kola'

This body of work was first awakened on the stolen lands of the Kaurna people; then written on the stolen lands of the Ngunnawal and Ngambri people. Sovereignty was never ceded. Cham Zhi Yi and Subbed In pay their respects to elders past and present. We extend warmth and solidarity to the Cadigal-Wangal people of the Eora Nation where this book was edited and designed, and the Wurundjeri people of the Kulin nation where this book was printed and bound.

Always was, always will be Aboriginal land.

8	untitled 1
10	colonisation 2 ways
13	zhi gets a poem tattooed at a neighbourhood studio
17	i mean to say
19	apparition
22	love by way of maccas
25	soak
28	be sure we aren't dreaming
30	portrait of forgiveness as lotus root
32	grandma goes live on facebook
36	untitled 2
38	post Solange
46	slept into the arvo dreaming of Beyoncé
48	to be forgiven here
50	ingatan
52	all the water of weereewa passes through
56	i dreamt of you again & this time you multiplied
58	what would it take to undream you
60	untitled 3
62	poem i enjoy more than i do him
64	throwaway lux
69	let me be survived by loneliness
74	in *Queer Eye* jonathan says this about regular old store bought shampoo
77	in *Salt, Fat, Acid, Heat* Samin Nosrat says
79	in *If You Are The One* 孟老师 says about you
81	blur by the
83	i had a dream in which i cried freely

Untitled 1

if i utter aloud everything that bores and agitates me about ▮▮▮▮ people · will that soften my severity

every weekend i go away for a long walk then tunnel into food conjuring haze · reemerge at peace · only to arrive here · white heat searing lens · i hate being told when to eat ▮▮▮▮▮▮▮▮ and more often · when not to what not to · i don't know if they boast of their wives' cooking-baking excellence because they · believe they possess these skills as their own · or if they are grateful to be well fed · by proximity to greatness · i don't like airing that i'm a good cook for fear that people would think i'd make a good wife · i am a good cook first and foremost for my survival · in turning ▮▮▮▮▮▮▮ into nourishment · what else am i to do with · all · this · gunky · mess · of · emotions · if not eat it

i had half an onion inked onto my thigh · a week in · between leaving home · and rolling my skirt up on the toilet · the skin scabbing over had turned ash grey like · being brought too close to the open flame of a bunsen burner · on a real onion · the flakes of skin would curl up and disintegrate · on this one · it is just my skin

colonisation
2 ways

brekkie

tryna figure out when i learnt the word
brekkie & when it crept into my vocabulary
to manifest autonomously tryna figure
out when i learnt the origin of soft
boiled to be *eggs & soldiers* & when i'd began
reliving it each time i sink eggs into bubbling
water somewhere between six & seven minutes later

    drain the pot crack the eggs drain the shells
think

       of the soldiers that could've been dipped
& put them out instead splash soy
sauce scatter white pepper bleed yolks
edible Pollock soaked into fluffy toast
spooned to mouth soft boiled dribble misses
peppered yolk-soy-whites on lip licked
savoured swallowed tear up more toast wipe
the bowl with salty slick brekkie eat

benny

you've heard this before
knife parting egg
yolk gushes
out
to mingle
with hollandaise
sunlight
pool
at foot of mountain
of bread
smoked salmon dark
yolk in shadow full
moon in clouds
set to work
on excavating
mountain drape drenched
muffin over mouth
oranged liquid oranged
body oranged love
on lip on chin on

nothing

is as sensual as before
it's been englished

zhi gets a poem tattooed at a neighbourhood studio

in the process of conceiving a tattoo
i become malleable, say
to the young white
who speaks in mimicked german accent

>okay
>what can i do
>to make this easier for you —
>move it to my back?

we unwind the loop i intended for the poem to become
restore it to the structure intended by the poet

>here —

guiding him along the wall of my back just
upon the blade of my shoulder, poem
be sinew
powering each movement of left arm

he sets screens up
i take my top off
he unhooks my bra
i sit front against back of chair, crouched

over tattoo bed
browse the interwebs as
he grazes needles against
cold skin

my mother pings me on whatsapp

        zhi yi
        you need anything from us
        to bring in june
        list it out

    nah just the blanket

reports to me
a line is complete

    we have time today

        no need mama

    baju? seluar?
    kaya

        no need la maybe kaya

ok

        tq mummy

pretend to give a shit about this white man's aspirations as he carves
musing onto my skin

    he tells me the story of how he got into tattooing
    does not ask about the poem

reports to me he is fixing up
little edges   okay

when he's done i go to the mirror
back bare in a studio full of white men
see inked poem on skin, say
this is perfect

he wraps my tattoo up
i say thank you
he hooks my bra back on
i say thank you

you know

this man spent a whole hour of his life attempting to stencil
this poem onto my arm & it kicks & drifts
garamond contorting & only then
onto my back & this

 is the last he sees of the poem —

> i wish i
> was the dream
> of ancestors
> and not
> the anarchy
> of descent*

   — this is the last i see of this white man
this is the first i see of the poem

---

*tattooed poem *Genealogy* by Craig Santos Perez

i mean to say

looking for something to pacify me from being idle so
i cut up a papaya & slot a wobbly orange unit into my
    mouth, suckle
i may only have two mouths, one for eating & the other
for this precise amount of ambiguous

liken dried flaked skin round edge of
lip to desiccated coconut
because even the lack of
moisture can be a revelation

                i am resistant to veganism
      the same reason
      a white person
      might reject the concept of
   race: the desire
      to participate in
tradition

for a snack crunch a sheet of roasted laver
in folding between fingers then wrap
tongue around, give water
this

is how it feels
to at once be exalted
by salt & devastate
the most delicate

apparition

waiting on the tv to roll into commercials
tell me my luck in the new year

re-educated in swagger at the mahjong table
pong! chee bellows & snatches

newly dispensed tile meet
it to two identical others

we pass round cookies & tarts as we pass rounds
& i am learning again how much alike

i am my mother
& how much i am not from grandaunties

i've read of women like my ma
[petite pretty women]

arriving in australia & am reminded that
i am not one of them

but we're all home now
aren't we?

isolate

into room [generation]
into room [location: origin]

into room [language]
into room [location: current]

into room [not
present] i

wanna go home; i wanna go home; come
spring i sing · spring wind she kisses

my cheek; i am going
home; i wanna come home —

have i missed

the exit?

love by way of maccas

for Kelvin Teo

i fkn love maccas · u should kno · after work
drive thru · sitting in the mouth of the order lane ·
chipped·faded lipstick wondering · if i'd go
for the dbl cheeseburger or qtr pounder or mcnuggets
coming up to my turn · letting the speaker
grained·nasalled voice wash

                        what can i get for you today?

over me · the inhuman sound · invokes
within me a truest desire · so much so
that · my response surprises · even myself

    10 pc mcnuggets in a large meal
    with ...

    oreo mcflurry pls

was i here for the mediocre yet exceptional joy
of   mcnuggets   or
some fkn ice cream · u kno
i been in this drive thru so many times that
shame · is a side that comes with my order but

    the first time i set foot inside this maccas
            it was with you

there are so many order stations now which gives
us the option not to interact with people but you
bypass them all & go straight to the counter say

two sausage & egg mcmuffins with
regular cap & small latte

grab a table near the tv · japanese gameshow playing child shredded by sobs on the table next to ours from being told to leave the play area by their mother · says

enough enough · here have some pancake

}} it is important to say she said this in mandarin
it is important to say we both understood her }}

the food gets here · we both reach first for the hash browns · you eat half & leave the rest wrapped in paper · i eat it all · we eat so fast · greased lips & fingers · down our coffees · then return to your hash brown · salt on caffeinated tongue · teeth to slightly deflated mush · crisp but not quite · you offer me a bite · i take it · i still don't understand why we don't order extra when · really · really really · it is what we want

soak

for Kelvin Teo

kin lok lai! jiak beng liao!

i scrape the sides of pot   rice
rolling   into curve of spoon
clumping

five portions —

seven   if 婆婆 & 公公 are staying with us

we eat   i stack the ceramics
           carry them to the sink
           wash them

no rice left
          i soap the pot to soak

lai. let's eat

you scrape the sides of pot   rice
rolling   into the curve of spoon
clumping

two portions —

four   if lisa & chris are joining us
we eat   you stack the dishes
         load the dishwasher
         wash them

the rice is cold now

you spoon it
                into a container

you soap the pot to soak

i scrape the sides of pot   rice
rolling   into curve of spoon
clumping

one portion

i eat   carry my plate
           to the sink
           wash it

the rice is cold now

i spoon it
                into a container

i soap the pot

                          soak

be sure we aren't dreaming

for 公公

my favourite ginger these days is blue, crushed & grated
for the briefest moment   the room smells just
like fresh steamed oh cheong 婆婆 makes

                                      if i grate
ginger in vicinity to this butterfly, will they take it to 公
公 in the underworld

                           we really didn't know one
another in living or in death   the difference was · in living
· i knew · he ate well · to be flushed
into the underworld is to dissipate pain
there · he walks freely repeat: he is now in the better
place

    i migrate in search of · the better life ·
here i will have free healthcare (capped) · the privilege of
paying $15 for roti & dahl & on weekends
the joy of picking my favorite foods from
the arsenal of freezers at the asian grocer's

                        ·

                in naming pain
impart ink to tucked away places of this
                   body · this
             is where they live
         give the whole of my sight
    away to light   allow myself
    the mourning of redacted history

                        ·

today's grace is finding space in my bathroom for green
today's devastation is the absence of entry for sunlight

maybe the plants i bring to this room
can live under heat lamp on weekdays &
out on the good place on weekends
don't we don't we don't we deserve this pinch in time ?

portrait of forgiveness as lotus root

for 婆婆

                    lotus root
                    said to be without flavor
                    absorbs everything it is exposed to
                    & becomes

five years   since i've left home   i soak
                    skin-on peanuts & red dates in water
                    watch them belly out
                    soften

in my wait   i brush the dirt from lotus root & peel
                    the skin off exposing
                    woody translucence

                    slice thick chunks
                    cover pork ribs with
                    pour over storm of peanuts
                    red dates

two hours   or whatever really we don't deal
                    precision to broth so long as the peanuts
                    disrobe · red dates turn themselves out to
                    surrender · pork fat gives itself in · to heat
                    & lotus root ·   lotus root

                    mutes its flesh brown to the colour of
                    time-enriched water

all this time   & sturdy still

grandma goes live on facebook

for 婆婆

i.

i was 18 when i moved to adelaide. for months, i took the bus at the end of my street on north terrace every other saturday and rode 40 minutes to go to ikea. all i wanted to do was walk. when i finally decided i could luxuriate, i stood in line at the cafeteria to grab meatballs. i've waited months for this. they were smaller than i know them to be but i still believed in them. but then i bit into one —

                        so it isn't as if i wasn't aware i'm not in the same country. it was just that i thought i could surive this

•

i don't eat at papparich when i'm in australia. i say it's because it's expensive and half the quality of what you get in malaysia — i'm not wrong but

•

i overhear my colleagues talk about ikea   *I've only been once.*
I'm sorry?!   i interjected
he looks up   *Why? Do you like going to Ikea?*
Yeah, it's really fun to go for a walk.

                        i wanted to laugh at myself
i mean to say
        Ikea is the same all over the world & reminds me of home   except the meatballs, except the meatballs

•

                          i caved and went to
papparich for roti telur bawang stared at the seaweed
green tiles lining the wall they are the green
on the batik my mother gave me

ii.

[i wish i had more people to eat with than just me]
] if i say this silently enough maybe i won't jinx myself
[more often than i'd like to admit [[because it's soft
of me to   ]]   i think of 婆婆 leaving me
the tender boned pork in broth] maybe
one day i'd be loved like this again }

iii.

there are two ways i've been entering my
grandmother's kitchen:

1.   in my dreams
2.   the internet

•

after the passing of my grandfather, pa got 婆婆 a
smartphone

and once

                she went live on facebook

honest to god, i thought she figured out how to work the internet and thought i was gonna get my grandma streaming cooking vids onto the webs

  she didn't, in fact, figure out how to use the internet

i entered the live cast and saw

3.   a lime green stool from ikea
4.   婆婆's shadow draped over it
5.   a floating pinky drawing upwards, moving down
6.
7.   and drawing upwards again
8.   looping,
9.   cast against white floor tiles
10.

Untitled 2

everything

i

hate

to

know

possess

nourishment

eat it

home

grey like   the open flame of

my skin

post Solange

for Saaro Umar

today
today i
today i watch
today i watch the lining
i watch the lining of my
watch the lining of my uterus
the lining of my uterus exit
of uterus exit my body
my uterus exit my body in
exit my body in a single
my body in a single unbroken
in a single unbroken thread
a single unbroken unbroken thread thread

today
i today
watch i today
the lining watch i today
of my the lining watch i
uterus of my the lining watch
exit uterus of my the lining
my body exit uterus of
in my body exit my uterus
a single in my body exit
unbroken a single in my body
thread unbroken a single in
thread unbroken thread a single unbroken

•

   the truth is

  it is less romantic than painting
dyeing my lips the colour of dried
blood caked onto sanitary pad   or
                                  if i were more polite

                 the colour
of dried wine on rim of glass but
                                i am not
                           &
                   i am telling you
i mean to be this vulgar or really

                                this truthful

              what else am i to do   with
                                      this moist southeast asian mouth
                                      withering here
                                      in the southern hemisphere
                         edge of   split-fraying
                                      loosening seatbelt like
                                      ready to disembark
                                      from this face
                               now   that i've stowed away
                                      four of my five tongues for winter
what else are they to do with me   ?

·

    post Solange
        you asked if we were better online
than off   i said
      maybe
    but i mean to say
        i am shy even
  especially
        with you &   need
    a minute
  twist
      my body sideways
            few ways
        to meet
  your wattle
    eyes over
        seat

          i love you
          & you know this

      discuss the planets & how ours
correspond & why
    we are cosmically delicious
    say again   we have not taken a photo together
        in two years of intimacy   if
      photographed   will our vividry
dissipate?

        i do not trust
        another eye
      on our
        transcendence

·

              when my mother tells the story of my birth
        she reminds me that the first time she laid eyes on me
her first feeling was disappointment   imagine
      gestating for nine months going into labour
                           all that trouble
              in the business of childbirth only
                       for your very first baby not to be
             everything
    you hoped for
             tells me your nose was squished
  undefined like mine wished
you had your dad's nose   imagine
     your daughter defying the genetics prescribed for her
                            your tall slender figure
               not reflected here
     fleshing outwards & outwards
jupiter dominated biology
       funhouse mirror like
                  learning to love this body

            - jk, but also v srsly -

       tfw ur a sag & sposed to be centaur but
       turn out more like faun   & choose
           for all of this to be
            so. damn. kewt.
      only to be told quarter century on how

             your too much
         is in fact just too much

     gestate a sensuality out this mess

      love her love her love her like
        if you choose   u kewt 2

·

complicated relationship with the word craft
i wish it wasn't so colonised that it keeps being said to keep
me out
i say i don't care for it
until a stranger named my praxis
& suddenly
my body necessitates immersion-obsession
all I require
is   freedom; the love of my life
tells me about
Eileen Myles
in an interview says
–   I want to be precise in this freedom   –
& truly I require for the process of precise naming
to be boundless
there is a lump in my throat the size of Saturn
crick in my neck like a hickey from our conversation
story you & I into forever
begin naming everything compulsively in order to arrive at
Accuracy; look forward
to never getting there

i can't tell
if i'm horny
or wanting
to write a poem
tell me again
how you said
well fuck me then
when i said
i want
to be with
a cap mars
gave me a
dry mouth
waiting
for you to
wet

·

i am running out of body so i keep a glass on my desk
that i drink out of for a week until the rim clouds with the
different shades of red of my lips i pour my selves into it
here is a vessel that may hold me

                                      undo my person
acne on cheeks scraped find exits on my face

            getting the fuck out

you begin calling me pockets here is a name for my
mutability where i am pockets what pockets i am
i am just pockets in your big big pocket all the pockets
missing you

                    a poem tucked between skin
                    and skull

                                  in my sleep
reminds me of her existence by dismantling roof
of mouth metamorphosise to blood when i wake drips
down riverbed tween front teeth hibiscus
red column

              we hold you up

                                  i leave my nails
to grow sharp as tip of waning crescent moon channel
Hekate i want to remember Ancience
excavate my skull from the wound in back of ear
descabbed white ash unbecome human
gram by gram what is skin but a vessel

slept into the arvo dreaming of Beyoncé

we're hanging out   out front of coles
talking about caramel popcorn
i tell her about johnny's
& go in to get her a bag
it's on sale
i am in line at the checkout when
Beyoncé comes looking for me
singing my name
as she does

•

my awake self struggles
with how i wasted Beyoncé's time with
caramel popcorn
or that i wasted my time with Beyoncé with
caramel popcorn
or that
caramel popcorn
is the most valuable thing i have to offer
& yet

Beyoncé
sings   my name
in search of me &
caramel popcorn

to be forgiven here

.

i am waiting
on a permutation of this city
where i run into you
in that time, collect
blood creeping from nail beds
in the hem of my sleeve
like a breath held

                                                     into this body of water i enter

my mother enjoys reminding me
of the fullness of my lips
& that i must hide them
tuck them in, she says
my mouth a pocket for ripened girlhood
i think ma thinks ripeness
is just a rot waiting to turn

put lipstick on
to attend a meal
broth washing upon
maroon-shored mouth
colour undressed
an unbecoming
becomes ritual

.

a boy
i could be the mother to
eyes me
like a ripe peach for the taking
i see
the wound on my lower lip growing
into a rift   red as worship

to this body of water i surrender

when i run into you · if
i told you i loved you · i think
it is nothing you haven't heard before
i know you
across the breadth of the stage
& you know me
across the breadth of my gaze

even then
this is more
than i would give
most people
i don't speak to you after
slip past you not unnoticed
leave · i have been strange enough

ingatan

in summer my nativity returns to me – sweat milked
from scalp · back · fold of arms · back of knees like
cling film; dyed all hues brown – caramelised-flavour
skin · hair mahogany · (so there they are   the eyes);

remembers hujan —
jika sempat · biarkan saja · kotak hati   kat spotify

breasts taut in turquoise-veined nets like pears clutched
in styrofoam · i take a blade to lower abdomen & carve
erasing first fine hairs then dead skin like eschars of razor's
edge · there begins the itch · stop stop stop · the mother

remembers home —
knuckles to mushrooms of blood sprouting from pores

tingles lower still – the girl hovers over stove · slides
chopped · scalded 五花肉 into pot · overdoes cloves
of garlic · always · pack of herbs · soy sauce · stirs —

remembers warmth —
the mother pats it down · nestles & waits for flood

all the water of Weereewa passes through

this is not a myth —

half an hour out the city of canberra, a lake
without outflow to other bodies of water
is known to empty
& fill
as they please

i.

fogging over Ngunnawal
in evenings make
this sky
baby blue sweet
like pulut tekan

picked *clitoria ternatea* soak
glutinous rice with, if i sink my teeth in

will grains wet
on my teeth my tongue waiting
to be eased down only
by kaya

ii.

i follow my gut onto mount ainslie
& return, convinced
i am here
because sunbathed wattle reminds me
of Saaro's eyes

but what do i know but
an obsession

iii.

go
to black mountain
who inhibits me
& knots
my insides

in my descent

gives blood

iv.

i tell people to call me zhi   but
truly my heart swells when

my mother says me whole

i want to know this joy daily
but cannot bear

the affliction of a name

v.

is weereewa empty?

                    or are we?

vi.

                                the malaysian anthem goes
negaraku, tanah tumpahnya darahku
my country, for this earth my blood spills

                      in welcome to country
learn the name of country in language say
                            dhaura

                           if   darah be blood

               dhaura be country

show me a future where i

                           become

                     both

i dreamt of
you again &
this time you
multiplied

i won't stop dreaming   of
permutations of you   &
permutations of us   in
permutations of spaces   i am a whole weeping thing

         you in that shade of blue
               shimmering velvet of it

my hips   (burgeoning   bracket)
my forearm   exclamation mark   tipped
my fingers   a string of periods like pearls cascading

            down down
                    love
momentously   fucked
   kill   anything   that   feels

string of periods like pearls   choke
the more i devoid   this fantasy of air
the more vivid it   becomes

    everything tightens
cling wrapped lemon
             suffocate then
spit   biled texts

what would it take to undream you

mimosa cradled hydrangeas
recede
mimosa eats hydrangeas
                        shame bearing grass
when i reach for   everything that survives
in the memory of   my childhood
becomes absence

Untitled 3

soften

into haze
· reemerge

more

grateful by proximity to
fear
i'd cook first
my survival ·
what else am i

home

to

poem i enjoy more than i do him

i want you to think i am proximate to magic if not magic herself
i am so mutable i believe i have come the closest i can
i have run out of tricks to surprise you with
i wish i would stop being tender & easily imprinted upon

because my body is a byproduct of reactions   i have adopted
make me feel as my anthem
the biggest turn on lies   in reciprocity
i begin to trust you with fragments of my poetry but i
overestimate a man's capacity at desire   you end

with my body   i earn a whiplash & a blush
i want to ask   what will you do to me
& be honey in your hands but
these sag thighs don't chase

part for pleasure
cure a bitterness with chai sweetened lips
fold spread   pucker
i enter myself before you   i must love you

throwaway lux

eat mango at the risk of a strand of its flesh threading
between teeth: marker for a thing worse than tenderness

in the entirety of my small bulbous adulthood   my name
has only once been naturalised, to the tongue of a boyfriend

of a housemate who no longer lives with me; if
a prayer occurs in airplane mode, will god hear me?

i learn to speak. curtly. shortly. wear bold lipstick & never
ever let scabs decease into skin

break it

        you need to break it to smell it

i pull apart a leaf by its spine & crush a smear of lovely
across my fingertips, blood smelling of something other than iron

bravely click disconnect & make a possibility of every mundane
do i spend my time lining my gums with clichés? or may i learn

to speak true —
truly, what does it take to recall a person into a language?   when
i left

i have no real means of returning to first
a girl travels home via flimsy kayak

on losing sight of shore (home or otherwise),
a panic diseased upon her limbs

limps her mind & leaves with her
at the end of this poem: good taste, mangoes &

numbness; some say she's still at sea swaying in excuses or
whatever. the source of her greatest frustration however

is that she has still yet to unthread mango flesh from
between her teeth & in reckless, charged attempts to dislodge

had bitten her tongue clean off

                              i am resistant to veganism
                  the same reason
                  a white person
                  might reject the concept of
         race: the desire
                  to participate in
tradition

let me be survived by loneliness

give two names to a stretch of space
my body
loved & lonely
(proximity or

proximity & distance
conveys the difference between
by her approximation to blood
distance)

in a dream   displace reams of staircases to outer space
dismantle from under each step its riser
open staircase be frame for stars
me on narrow step leading descent of

                              an uncle a brother a cousin my mother

— how does anyone summon anything remotely close to courage or will to execute even mindless routine when breathing becomes an impossibility i think about how easy it is to put one foot out & let gravity take me to the next step, the landing, the next set (i know what i know what is gravity in outer space & what is home where there is exile

               this here is a dream this is post-something or -another this bears no
                                                                         consequence)

                              i want nothing to have me · including gravity

where does this lead us?

i contemplate the stacks & stacks of stairs under me without the punctuation of floors
think of hell, all eighteen levels
think of levels 层 oddly 尸 body (dead) above cloud 云

where does this leave us?

when i wake i set about cutting & bruising anything that bleeds tears
cook everything that stings
begin eating a meal that will satiate my hunger before it does my nostalgia
put away the leftovers
call ma

ma i am wanting. i am wanting to go home. let home be as simple as proximity to you. home need not be Swatow

— & because this poem is for a white audience let me clarify Swatow is the city in Guangzhou where generations ago my family was "from". before australia. before malaysia. & generations before Swatow we must have been from elsewhere but my longing for this specific city stems from a fantasy: that no one in Swatow ever asked our ancestors "where are you from?" —

      ma can i come home?   the only indigeneity i recognise   is to you

when did white arrive on the shores of time?

   she too has been colonised

      expel white from spine

         let it be ash

      convince myself   despite my location   my ancestors

all their trades their tongues their gods & their ghosts be   my legacy

       remind myself   i am many

         pray   this lonely survives me

if i bend my wrists out they look just
like the soles of my feet which are
as vulnerable or as tough as the other
or both

in *Queer Eye* Jonathan says about this regular old store bought shampoo

the ingredients that are in this are not working
sodium lauryl sulfate
which is literally the same thing that cleans
the carburettor of a car

                                                                                     wow

it is hard. core.
it is literally like an AK47 y'know
it's not gentle.

·

shampoo you've used your whole life, thinking: this cleans & you consider no other option but then you move on · try organic natural products & shit

        you realise
                nourishment *is* possible

of course this perspective does not come about until you think, hey — if i go back to that old shampoo i could save so much money (or whatever other reason(s) you'd return to old shampoos). it was not *that* bad, was it? so you go back to that shit & your hair dries out instantaneously. in shock at what you're willing to do to yourself so · it really *was* that bad

·

it now seems sensible to return to your organic natural things. but this shampoo. *this* shampoo somehow manages to convince you that maybe you do need cleansing like you're the carburettor of a car · if & when this happens get a pump of that organic natural goodness & slather

i beg of you

remind yourself · nourishment is possible & you are deserving because · look · no shampoo in the world can decide for you · you are a grown woman you choose your own fkn shampoos in *Salt, Fat, Acid, Heat* Samin Nosrat says

i'm sorry grandma
before sliding
into her mouth

looking skywards
a linen white strip of pork fat
i swear i saw tears

in *If You Are The One* 孟老师 says about you

if you do anything purely because your parents told you to & you do not like the outcome, you have no one to blame but yourself because you have not chosen to become an independent person

•

omg ma see?? even 孟老师 says you shouldn't force me to do things. i need to become an independent person.　}{　oh i know i can't force you to do anything anymore you're a completely different person now

•

:: i want to say & yet you try. so hard. so unrelentingly that i am suffocating but instead i say ::

good.

blur by the

said	you	i
	you have communication issues now	i've always had it
meant	who are you	
		you've never known me · i didn't know myself

·

i started out thinking i knew what needed to be said but the truth is i don't remember anything save for 1. the above · 2. me locked in the bathroom catching my breath · 3. you wanting to leave the house · 4. me screaming IT'S NOT A PERSONAL ATTACK. IT'S NOT A PERSONAL ATTACK · 4. me in the dark · 4. you a blur by the counter · 4. me leaving the house · 4. two magpies landing closer to me than they ever had

· singing

i had a dream
in which i cried
freely

i had a dream	in which i cried freely
	& have only just recalled
this	to be just a dream & not in fact
real	
once	my impulse carried me to a tree
	which i climbed
	& melted
	into the cradled elbow of
where	i had a dream
	in which i cried freely
water	a nectar
perforates	the myth of insolvency
	of an earth moon
	i am told
	i can do better but why
	can't the imperfection of the current be
its own	good

ACKNOWLEDGEMENTS

My most immense gratitude
To Dan, Victoria and Egg, for this gift;
To Winter Tangerine, for the workshops *Sing That Like Dovesong* and *To Carry Within Us An Orchard, To Eat* — without which the poems *post Solange*, *all the water of Weereewa passes through* and *grandma goes live on facebook* would not have been birthed;
To Toolkits, for the 2016 cohort -
        most especially, for Saaro Umar;
To Saaro Umar, for our blood;
To Kelvin Teo, for the water;
To my family, for Everything; and
To Ngunnawal and Ngambri country, for the sight.
All my love.

'zhi gets a poem tattooed at a neighbourhood studio' first published in *daikon* zine*; 'apparition' first published in *Longing for Home zine*; 'soak' & 'ingatan' first published in *Pencilled In Issue #1*; 'to be forgiven here' first published in *Tell Me Like You Mean It Vol. 2*; 'poem i enjoy more than i do him' & 'i mean to say' (previously 'parched') first published in *Ibis House*; 'throwaway lux' first published in *The Suburbam Review Issue #11*.

ABOUT THE AUTHOR

Zhi is a Malaysian woman currently based on Ngunnawal and Ngambri country which now exists as the esoteric wormhole known as Canberra. She is a believer of deep joy mediocrity and aspires to full time tenderness. She is best digitised on instagram *@chamzhiyi*.

ABOUT SUBBED IN

Subbed In is a not-for-profit DIY literary organisation and small press based in Sydney, Australia. Subbed In's program of publications and events aim to elevate the voices of trans people, people of colour, non-binary people, sex workers, women, people with a disability, LGBTQIA+ people, First Nations people, survivors, working class people, and anyone who finds themselves on the margins of the supremely white, cis, heteronormative, capitalist, colonial, ableist, patriarchal hellscape in which we live.

For more information visit: *www.subbed.in*

ALSO AVAILABLE FROM SUBBED IN

When I die slingshot my ashes onto the surface of the moon
by Jennifer Nguyen

HAUNT (THE KOOLIE)
by Jason Gray

The Hostage
by Šime Knežević

If you're sexy and you know it slap your hams
by Eloise Grills

wheeze
by Marcus Whale

Parenthetical Bodies
by Alex Gallagher

The Naming
by Aisyah Shah Idil

Girls and Buoyant
by Emily Crocker

Uncle Hercules and other lies
by Patrick Lenton

www.ingramcontent.com/pod-product-compliance
Lightning Source LLC
Chambersburg PA
CBHW032047290426
44110CB00012B/993